CONTE

Poetry Book Society

CHOICE RECOMMENDATION SPECIAL COMMENDATION SELECTORS	SANDEEP PARMAR & VIDYAN RAVINTHIRAN
TRANSLATION SELECTOR	GEORGE SZIRTES
PAMPHLET SELECTORS	A.B. JACKSON & DENISE SAUL
WILD CARD SELECTOR	ANTHONY ANAXAGOROU
CONTRIBUTORS	SOPHIE O'NEILL NATHANIEL SPAIN SAM BUCHAN-WATTS LEDBURY CRITICS & STUDENTS
EDITORIAL & DESIGN	ALICE KATE MULLEN

Membership Options

Associate - *4 bulletins a year* (UK £18, Europe £20, Overseas £23)

Full - *4 Choice books & 4 bulletins a year* (£55, £65, £75)

Charter - *4 Choices, 16 Recommendation books & 4 bulletins* (£170, £185, £215)

Education - *4 Choice books, 4 bulletins & teaching notes* (£58, £68, £78)

Charter Education - *4 Choice books, 16 Recommendation books, 4 bulletins, posters & teaching notes* (£180, £195, £225)

Translation - *4 Recommended Translations & 4 bulletins* (£70, £100, £118)

Student - *4 Choice books & 4 bulletins* (£27, £47, £57)

Single copies £5

Cover Art Emma Holliday. 'Longsands Looking North'. www.emmaholliday.co.uk

Copyright Poetry Book Society and contributors. All rights reserved.

ISBN 9781999858926 ISSN 0551-1690

Supported using public funding by
ARTS COUNCIL ENGLAND

Poetry Book Society | Inpress Books | Churchill House | 12 Mosley Street |
Newcastle upon Tyne | NE1 1DE | 0191 230 8100 | pbs@inpressbooks.co.uk

WWW.POETRYBOOKS.CO.UK

LETTER FROM THE PBS

We are delighted to announce Vahni Capildeo's *Venus as a Bear* as the Summer Choice. The poet selectors were impressed with Capildeo's "verbal and intellectual voracity". The Recommendations take us to Puerto Rico with Loretta Collins Klobah's collection, *Ricantations*, all about her "island home", Tishani Doshi reveals the moment of inspiration for *Girls Are Coming Out of the Woods*, a moving exploration of rape and gender violence set alongside poems about coastal life on the Bay of Bengal. Faisal Mohyuddin explores intergenerational trauma in *The Displaced Children of Displaced Children*, "a deeply necessary, clear and moving rejoinder to the silence of all our histories." Alice Miller is praised for her "genuinely unpredictable" works in *Nowhere Nearer*.

Michael O'Neill and John Kinsella receive Special Commendations for their collections, the selectors praise O'Neill for the faith in humanity which shines through his poetry and Kinsella for his call to change as a poet-activist. Austrian poet Evelyn Schlag's *All Under One Roof* wins the tight fought contest for Recommended Translation, translated with a "lightness of touch" by Karen Leeder, both of whom will be reading at our Northern Poetry Symposium on 3rd May. Having heard Mary Jean Chan read at the Forward Prize, I am delighted she has been awarded the Pamphlet Choice with *A Hurry of English*. Amy Key's *Isn't Forever* is our first-ever Wild Card Choice and we look forward to seeking out future boundary-pushing collections.

We hope you enjoy reading the winning poems from the PBS Student Poetry Prize – we are delighted to be supporting emerging poets as well as celebrating more established poets in our selections. Thanks also to the Ledbury Emerging Poetry Critics, curated by PBS Book Selector Sandeep Parmar and our Newcastle University student contributors for their excellent guest reviews in this issue.

We look forward to launching the Summer *Bulletin* at our Northern Poetry Symposium with NCLA and Poettrios at Sage Gateshead on the 3rd May, as part of the Newcastle Poetry Festival. We're also delighted to feature this cover artwork from the Festival's Painter-in-Residence, Emma Holliday. Finally, we hope to see you at our PBS Summer Showcase at the Southbank on 25th July, featuring Sandeep Parmar, Amy Key, Mary Jean Chan and our student prize winner Jay G. Ying. Visit our website or subscribe to Alice's newsletters for more details.

- Sophie O'Neill, PBS and Inpress Director

VAHNI CAPILDEO

Vahni Capildeo works with multilingualism, place and memory. Their books include *Venus as a Bear* (Carcanet, 2018), *Measures of Expatriation* (Forward Poetry Prizes Best Collection, 2016) and *Utter* (Peepal Tree Press, 2013). Capildeo served as the Chair of the OCM Bocas Poetry Prize 2018 (Bocas Litfest, Trinidad & Tobago). They are a contributing advisor to *Blackbox Manifold*. Collaborations include intersemiotic translation with Chris McCabe for Zoë Skoulding's AHRC-funded 'Expanded Translation' (University of Bangor), and feminist theatre with Sophie Seita's collective, 'Gorgonia'. They are the Douglas Caster Cultural Fellow in Poetry at the University of Leeds.

VENUS AS A BEAR

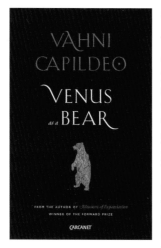

CARCANET | £9.99 | PBS PRICE £7.50

Vahni Capildeo's *Venus as a Bear* begins with an epigraph from Gertrude Stein's cubist-inspired poems from *Tender Buttons*. In Stein's 'A Piece of Coffee', Capildeo concludes: "supposing that there was no astonishment, is it not necessary to mingle astonishment." To take the object as itself, to return the thing to its referents, its many particulars, is partly also the poet's project here. Thus Capildeo liberates subjects from their field of language and discourse. This especially occurs with linguistic ingenuity in the book's sections entitled 'Creatures', 'Shameless Acts of Ekphrasis' and, finally, in 'Some Things', where Capildeo transforms moss into language itself: resistant, absorbing, ageless. Capildeo denies the lyrical fallacy of anthropomorphism, decentres the human eye for another, one that survives in abrupt bursts of Steinian syntax:

Don't slip. Grab the balustrade. Don't slip. She's broken her arm. Don't scrape too much off. It's beautiful. Bleach it all off. It's a risk. Coexist. Moss exists.

And, of course, Capildeo is mindful that objects are not apolitical, to be held at arm's length or fetishized. Stein's famous line "a rose is a rose is a rose"– an attempt to defamiliarize the symbol with its sign – is reworked in 'Heirloom Rose, for Maya':

[…] the reddest rose nonetheless a blonde princess, dangerous, dangerous to me, rose of heritable identity, not flaming shedding transgressing parterres and pathways not rose phénix rose curieuse but emblem of empire, imperial as natural, pressing away the senses' write/right to come to the rose as is – you could even make wars under its banner, york or lancaster, roses, rose is, rose isn't, sorry Gertrude Stein, rose exceeds/is in excess of no I mean is exceeded by connotations, with heirloom, of 'rose'.

Here the heirloom rose, prized for its pure origins, is the bloodiest perennial in the imperial garden. With characteristic verbal and intellectual voracity, Capildeo remakes the seen world for us and, in doing so, astonishes.

SANDEEP PARMAR

VAHNI CAPILDEO

The working title for *Venus as a Bear* was *Some Things*, and the inspiration for the book was exactly that. This is a book of encounters with it-ness; not images, stories or arguments. The poems are (for me) unusually small and poem-looking. Offering spaces of stillness, dwelling *with* rather than *on* their subjects, perhaps they suggest ways for readers to recollect and explore emotionally what it's like to be, simply, in the presence of vibrant unknowability.

They arise from my having been intensely co-present with objects, places, creatures and languages, for example on the see-the-sea-both-sides island Inishbofin at Peadar King's Inishfest; or with Colin Graham and Selina Guinness at Tibradden as they looked after their lambs; or sitting with my feet on a floor of lipstick, rainbow, neon-bright installed stripes in Edinburgh's Fruitmarket Gallery; or remembering childhood in Port of Spain, condensed milk boiling on a gas stove with irregular, blue and orange flames. Their ground is a curious childhood: "playtime" with spiders and moss; reading grown-up books, alone; wondering and pondering over the "rapports" that Diderot anatomized between the beautiful and the beholder – Gertrude Stein and Francis Ponge came later.

It's possible to do a walkaround of the "itness" in *Venus as a Bear*; but is this an "inside" or an "outside", a seacoast or a cabinet? My previous full-length books presented themselves to me as waves and sequences; thickness, thinness, musical progression. This one, a book of things, feels different. The all-over, arresting quiver caused by what mutely and unmovedly commands my loving attention evidences the deep response which puts forth a poetry of filaments, forms of expression which exceed and confoundingly simplify an author's design or desire to reach a reader or "treat" a "topic". There can be both fascination and identification with the sense of "it".

VAHNI RECOMMENDS

Chairing the OCM Bocas Prize for Caribbean Poetry, with fellow judges Loretta Collins Klobah and Danielle Legros Georges, focuses my recommendations. We shortlisted living legend Kamau Brathwaite's *Liviticus*; Sonia Farmer's *Infidelities*, an artist's book about the gender-bending pirate Anne Bonny; Shara McCallum's *Madwoman*, which grabs at stereotypes like dance partners, reasoning with the spacey page; commended Andre Bagoo's tough and iridescent *Pitch Lake*; and admire the bloody, beautiful courage of Shivanee Ramlochan's *Everyone Knows I am a Haunting* (not entered, as Shivanee is Festival staff).

I CHOICE

8

SEED, FOR MAYA

I.   the voice of the seed

II.   you said

III.   as yet it has no voice

IV.   the seed
          perhaps ever

V.   a star, a trap, a tropism, a keep,
          a wrinkle, a tide; these voiced weirds; (k)not
          so sweet stone, so liquid seed

BJÖRK / BIRCH TREE

Take out the silver and the pallor, come out
from under ether, from being reasonable,
come down from being condemned to live behind clouds.
Lady into swan, come down; swan into sea,
set down; fire from the sea, set out; reach; launch.

In the winter in the square near Kjarvalsstaðir,
the only colour burns on birch tree torsos
intense as tribal scars, roughed up like embers,
natural-unnatural mineralic orange;
a silent whiteness whitely dark in daytime,
in self-lit snowlight witness to increasing night,
the birch trees in the square near Kjarvalsstaðir.

Lady into swan, the Icelandic moon is rising
on fourteen kinds of moss, on military
exercises, on the spire people leap from
whose stories may outlast the night. A tribute
is a summons; but who summons trees? They mean suspense,
an ending between chase and chase. Trees grow in pursuit.
A tribute is a summons; but who dismisses trees?
With the moon, a roaring rises, swatting at the air.

LORETTA COLLINS KLOBAH

Loretta Collins Klobah's first book *The Twelve Foot Neon Woman* (Peepal Tree Press, 2011) received the OCM Bocas Prize for Caribbean Literature for poetry and was shortlisted for the Felix Dennis Forward Prize for Best First Collection. She has been awarded the Pushcart Prize, the Earl Lyons Award from The Academy of American Poets and the Pam Wallace Award for an Aspiring Woman Writer. Her poems have been widely published in journals and anthologies. She lives in San Juan, Puerto Rico, where she is a Professor of Caribbean Literature and Creative Writing at the University of Puerto Rico.

RICANTATIONS

PEEPAL TREE | £9.99 | PBS PRICE £7.50

The title's a wordplay: it combines "Puerto Rican" with "incantations", and is also cross-linguistically enlivened by Spanish: the verb "cantar" means to "sing". Reading this collection, we also discern the shadowier presence of lamentations, following the devastation of the island by Hurricanes Irma and María. Klobah's poems tend towards narrative, scene-setting and vivid description.

Miguel's boat is tied to a mangrove pier
under ilán-ilán trees by the bay.
He used to carry me through the city
on inland waterways, trawling canals
that pass under low bridges, through mangroves,
where fishermen hurl hoop-nets from the bank,
and crabs roost on overhanging branches,

You want to know what happens next. But this momentum never upends or disfigures the poetic line. Each detail matters, and Klobah is concerned with displaced lives, like that of Eugenia Martínez Vallejo, the subject – or victim? – of Juan Carreño de Miranda's baroque paintings. One is called, like the poem, 'La Monstrua Desnuda', and invites the viewer to gawp at this court-creature:

In each grabby, hoggish hand,
she holds a red apple, quenchless
hunger of the Spanish Empire
embodied in one girl.
[…]
Carlos II had no children.
Were there children at the court
to pinch her and pull her around
by her red hair-ribbons?
Weakened by Prader-Willi,
if she fell asleep under a window,
did someone lug her to bed?

The adjectives are brutal: they capture the painter's gaze. Klobah turns Eugenia back from a symbol into a human being. Her language is cold and clear and wakened into vibrating life by the use, always, of the exact, terrible word: "did someone lug her to bed?" A relatively unheightened and documentarian style leaves open to moments like these, the sudden, poisonous glimmer of black ice.

VIDYAN RAVINTHIRAN

LORETTA COLLINS KLOBAH

Narrative poems in *Ricantations* travel from Britain to Jamaica, California, and Mexico. However, the majority are about my island home, Puerto Rico. It gave me enormous pleasure to work on this collection because of how dynamic, imaginative, varied and unexpected the material was and the challenges of using precise language in English and occasional Spanish. The book is inhabited by mythic creatures, animals, and anomalous beings – such as a flying gargoyle, a man wearing a Green Lantern suit at his wake, a Spanish Baroque girl with hyperphagia, and a family of high-wire walkers – so some poems read like speculative tales. Yet, even those marvellous in premise portray the realities of a colonised society ransacked by debt, mass migration and hurricanes.

When Samuel Lind provided *Ángel Plenero* for the cover art, while I was still drafting, *Ricantations* began to coalesce into a meaningful book. It symbolises societal resurrection through cultural arts inherited from ancestors, renewed and projected into the future: "The breaking of the stone symbolises how dynamic we are. We are Angels in a continuous, ongoing practice of culture" (Lind). *Ricantations* would have been impossible without my engagement with the long-standing literary and musical traditions of the English and Spanish-speaking Caribbean.

Poems address gender and narcoculture violence, but a surprising aspect of writing *Ricantations* was its focus on masculinity, portraying men whom I respect for how they follow their passions without causing harm: an ex-convict custodian of a butterfly farm; an artist who paints a pueblo, built by coffee barons, back into the green mountainside; an astronomer who dreams of a solarium where children can view the sun; a man who builds his space saucer house from ashtrays; a handyman who plays baseball with a boy in a leprosy colony; a calypso king; and a sculptor of the African orisha Osain among others.

LORETTA RECOMMENDS

Vahni Capildeo, *Venus as a Bear* (Carcanet) and *Measures of Expatriation* (Carcanet); Shivanee Ramlochan, *Everyone Knows I am a Haunting* (Peepal Tree Press); Danielle Boodoo-Fortuné, *Doe Songs* (Peepal Tree Press); John Robert Lee, *Collected Poems* (Peepal Tree Press); Ann-Margaret Lim, *Kingston Buttercup* (Peepal Tree Press); Melissa Lozada-Oliva, *Peluda* (Button Poetry); Vincent Toro, *Stereo. Island. Mosaic* (Ahsahta Press); Raquel Salas Rivera, *The Tertiary* (Timeless, Infinite Light).

Even as an angel, he had to take little hops

Image: *Angel Plenero* by Samuel Lind

THE GREEN LANTERN Y LOS MUERTOS SENTA'OS

There's a club in Heaven
for all the puertorriqueños
who had a Ché Guevara t-shirt
in their closets when they died.

Sometimes Ché, himself, rides
on a float in their annual parade.
Every year, though, Carlos Cabrera
wins the title of *Coolest Ché-Impersonator*.

He gained his bantam-weight angel wings when
some cabrón clubbed his noggin with a baseball bat,
though his family catalogued the event as an accident.

At the wake, he sat up – sort of – meditating
with the incense of a half-smoked cigarette
that sagged from his fingers, his hands
on his knees, his legs hard-wired
into a Buddha pose, a Ché beret cap
with its lone silver star on his beat-up head,
his stitched eyes concealed by black sunglasses.

It is true that his head drooped,
out-of-alignment from the bat strikes.
He did look cool, though, during his night vigil
in the basketball court of Caserío San José,
but after that, his wired legs never straightened out.
Even as an angel, he had to take little hops,
like a levitating yogi, to circumambulate Kingdom Come.

TISHANI DOSHI

Tishani Doshi is an award-winning writer and dancer of Welsh-Gujarati descent. She publishes fiction, poetry and essays. Her debut collection, *Countries of the Body*, won the Forward Prize for Best First Collection in 2006. She is also the recipient of an Eric Gregory Award and winner of the All-India Poetry Competition. In 2012 she published *Everything Begins Elsewhere* (Bloodaxe Books). Her most recent collection, *Girls Are Coming Out of the Woods* (Bloodaxe Books), deals with coastal life, gender violence, memory, happiness, ageing and the point of poetry. She lives on a beach in Tamil Nadu, India, with her husband and three dogs.

GIRLS ARE COMING OUT OF THE WOODS

BLOODAXE | £9.95 | PBS PRICE £7.47

Mortality and violence, in particular in the lives of women, pervade Tishani Doshi's third collection, *Girls Are Coming Out of the Woods*. From references to the everyday dangers of walking in public, to rape and femicide in India and beyond, as well as the subtle ageing process, these poems incantate with chilling candour. In 'Everyone Loves a Dead Girl' Doshi upbraids society's moral hypocrisy in turning a blind eye to violence against women: "In the parties of the real world, people talk about how some / girls walk down the wrong roads and fall down rabbit holes."

The collection's title poem hauntingly conjures these women seeking justice from the liminal silence of death, the marginal woods. Their voices make "such a noise, it's impossible / to hear" as they clear the ground and make way for their stories to be told. It is a bold and timely warning repeated throughout the book, even when the lyric subject takes the shape of a woman who resists the pressures of marriage, motherhood, even national identity.

The poems' speaker glides across borders, encountering the body as a non-negotiable space needing protection, even in spaces otherwise familiar and safe. In 'Monsoon Poem', Doshi takes aim at her readers' expectations of eroticised, diluvial landscapes: mangoes, jasmine and lotus flowers. She instead points to the ordinary, the unsightly, the deadly. The directness of Doshi's language often operates with an ironic humour, too, even at its most serious. Re-imagining Elizabeth Bishop's 'In the Waiting Room' in Madras, and its central epiphany of mortality, Doshi refocuses urgently not on how the self sees its death fearfully in violence elsewhere, but on the vulnerable themselves, the forgotten women objectified by our gaze.

> And what can be said about darkness after all?
> About men who board buses with iron rods?
> What can be said about all the dragging and laying
> of bodies to earth? Of landfills of lacerated breasts
> and vaginal scree, of girls hanging from a mango tree?

SANDEEP PARMAR

TISHANI DOSHI

I was on a bus in Southwest Ireland, passing these tremendous forests, listening to Bollywood music, and perhaps it was something about the disconnect, but I began to see armies of girls and women storm out of the woods. Some had panties around their lips, some were carrying iron bars. They were unstoppable, and they were coming. It was July 2013, seven months after Jyoti Singh had been raped on a bus in New Delhi. Everything had been overturned. Rape, a word that had skittered around the edge of conversations, suddenly became a battle cry. Like Neruda's "Come and see the blood in the streets!" we, in India, were shouting, "Come and see the rape in the streets!"

This collection isn't just about gender violence, although in the wake of the #MeToo campaign, some of the poems certainly herald the zeitgeist. But there are also poems about coastal life – the fragility of "orphaned slippers, styrofoam, fossil of crab," dead dogs and the rotting carapace of a turtle awash on the shore, fishermen with their tomb-sized chests, doorjambs plump with rain. The Bay of Bengal is a constant backdrop, hissing, whispering: "If everything we've lost were to return / with the sea, how simply we could offer / our sun-scarred lives, our soiled mattresses."

There are odes to one's first white hairs and Patrick Swayze's buttocks, instructions on how to be happy in 101 days, meditations on motherhood and mortality, poems of travel – pig-killing in Viet Hai, meeting Elizabeth Bishop in Madras, contemplating nakedness in a sauna in Gwangju. And there are poems that reiterate and insist on beauty and poetry and love. "I offer you my skin, / which is the same as offering you the / universe that breathes wild, through leather, / that sews our stomachs to gunny bags of / love. Always and only is a poem about love."

TISHANI RECOMMENDS

Books I'm looking forward to: *Luck is the Hook* by Imtiaz Dharker (Bloodaxe); *playtime* by Andrew McMillan (Cape), *Venus as a Bear* by Vahni Capildeo (Carcanet); *Calling a Wolf a Wolf* by Kaveh Akbar (Penguin); *Chan* by Hannah Lowe (Bloodaxe); *Soho* by Richard Scott (Faber); *House of Lords and Commons* by Ishion Hutchinson (Faber); *The Glass Aisle* by Paul Henry (Seren); *Brood* by Rhian Edwards (Seren).

RECOMMENDATION

And what can be said about darkness after all?

Image: Daria Petrilli

A FABLE FOR THE 21ST CENTURY

Existing is plagiarism.
                    E.M. CIORAN

                    There is no end to unknowing.
We read papers. Wrap fish in yesterday's news,
spread squares on the floor so puppy can pee
on Putin's face. Even the mountains cannot say
what killed the Sumerians all those years ago.
And as such, you should know that blindness
is historical, that nothing in this poem will make
you thinner, richer, or smarter. Myself –
I couldn't say how a light bulb worked,
but if we threw you headfirst into the past,
what would you say about the secrets
of chlorophyll? How would you expound
on the aggression of sea anemones,
the Battle of Plassey, Boko Haram?
Language is a peculiar destiny.
                    Once, at the desert's edge,
a circle of pilgrims spoke of wonder –
their lives dark with mud and hoes.
They didn't know you could make perfume
from rain, that human blood was more fattening
than beer. But their fears were ripe and lucent,
their clods of children plentiful, and God
walked among them, knitting sweaters
for injured chevaliers. Will you tell them
how everything that's been said is worth
saying again? How the body is helicoidal,
spiriting   on   and   on
How it is only ever through the will of nose,
bronchiole, trachea, lung,
that breath outpaces
any sadness
of tongue

| TISHANI DOSHI

ALICE MILLER

Alice Miller is a writer from New Zealand based in Berlin. She is the author of *Nowhere Nearer* (Pavilion and Auckland University Press) and *The Limits* (Shearsman and Auckland University Press). Alice is a graduate of the Iowa Writers' Workshop and the International Institute of Modern Letters, and was recently a fellow at the Akademie Schloss Solitude in Stuttgart. *Blaue Stunde*, an edition of her poems with a German translation, was published by Edition Solitude in 2016.

NOWHERE NEARER

Nowhere
Nearer

ALICE
MILLER

PAVILION POETRY | £9.99 | PBS PRICE £7.50

I was touched by Alice Miller's 'Observatory' – how it places a curious thought in a landscape, unstably:

Across from the observatory,
under cream cloud, what is it
death does when it undoes – the gradual unravel of a brain,
or a switch's flick to click off thought?

Immediacy, and pathos: "Young boys run past, serious for their bodies, / and in a breath of heat and sweat they're gone"; "Are you there, a man says into his phone. / A magnificent storm is coming." It's like thinking out loud, but with artful jump-cuts, and an ear for the tingling phrase. Or, for what Wordsworth experienced as a "gentle shock of mild surprise":

Since you left me I walk around here a lot.

I'm not dead, either. To be not dead,
I claim, is the most marvellous thing in the world.
Or to be touched, to have a finger pushed inside you.
Some people are approaching in Chinese dragon masks,
and twisting their way through a rehearsal. People hold their
scripts and do not know their hands shake.

- 'How to Remember'

Miller's poems seem always susceptible – their arcs can be injured into new shapes, they are not set in their ways, or dully prefabricated. There's a compelling, vulnerable person inside this poem: and so much more. She's willing to follow an impulse wherever it leads. To go so far, and no further; to turn aside, and notice something else. These poems are genuinely unpredictable, a rare thing, and their momentary stances or voice-postures have about them an air of irrepressible fiat. They can be epigrammatic – "A match strikes between / what we feel for those we know and / the bewilderment of strangers" – but often refuse the consolations of knowledge, exploding the urge to wallpaper the world with tedious explanation.

VIDYAN RAVINTHIRAN

ALICE MILLER

I return again and again to William James' notion that "Truth happens to an idea," that an idea "becomes true, is made true by events." What does this process of becoming true feel like? What kind of song does it make?

These poems explore the circularity of thought, the company of the dead, and the lure of alternative futures.

The book was written over several years of living in Vienna. A haunted city, Vienna tries to write its own past. It prefers to remember itself as the centre of an enormous empire. I thought a poet might also adopt this approach: to choose her ghosts, to write her own future, to cast herself as the protagonist. Of course, other pasts keep erupting, other voices and cities interrupt, unwelcome ghosts argue from the dead. Inside and outside the city, these poems trace a rise in political unrest and the collapse of a relationship. Like Calvino's Venice, Vienna becomes every city and no city, written by the memories of the people who glimpse it. It is a city of the dead – impossible to capture, and at the same time, impossible to escape.

I've always been fascinated (and occasionally paralysed) by the swirling counterfactual possibilities inherent in all our decisions. In a way this book could be described as an attempt to let our counterfactual existences live: to forge those counter-narratives – our seemingly false futures – into a needed strand of the story, an essential part of the ongoing process of becoming true.

ALICE RECOMMENDS

Some recent books I've enjoyed are: Nuar Alsadir, *Fourth Person Singular* (Pavilion Poetry); Alan Felsenthal, *Lowly* (Ugly Duckling); Joan Murray, *Drafts, Fragments, and Poems: The Complete Poetry* (Ed. Farnoosh Fathi, New York Review of Books); Lisa Samuels, *Symphony for Human Transport* (Shearsman); Zach Savich, *Daybed* (Black Ocean).

| RECOMMENDATION

It never lasts, didn't we know already?
It keeps not lasting.

THE LEVER

I spend hours as a gambler shovels coins
in whatever currency we keep

letting all our hours sleep
in the unbreakable brains of our machines.

When I pull the lever I know the lever.

I know each second before each second knows
me, but while I think this doubles me

I'm halved. When I pull
the lever I know the lever

pulls me; so I say the lever
has to do with love; because I want

to know you but know your being
makes me half-sad you're wholly here,

half-happy. I'm here to collect matter
that will let us build a new life. Still;

as the advertisements know,
there's nothing to it.

I ask for one more day, and it comes.

FAISAL MOHYUDDIN

Faisal Mohyuddin's debut full-length poetry collection, *The Displaced Children of Displaced Children* (Eyewear), was selected by Kimiko Hahn as winner of the 2017 Sexton Prize for Poetry. The author of the chapbook *The Riddle of Longing* (Backbone Press, 2017), he is the recipient of Prairie Schooner's Edward Stanley Award and a Gwendolyn Brooks Poetry Prize. An alumnus of the U.S. Department of State's Teachers for Global Classrooms program, he teaches English at Highland Park High School in Illinois, serves as an educator adviser to the global not-for-profit Narrative 4 and lives with his family in Chicago.

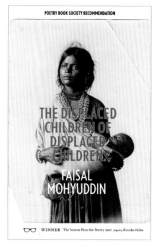

EYEWEAR | £10.99 | PBS PRICE £8.25

Faisal Mohyuddin's collection speaks to the rippling intergenerational trauma that originates in India's Partition, hastily orchestrated by the British Empire, and is sustained by subsequent migrations westwards since. Mohyuddin's poems locate the wound from which nostalgia or paranoia embeds itself in the psyche of future generations; through a series of traditional and expanded forms ranging from the ghazal to the prose poem, he commemorates, retells, draws parallels between revolution and despair. Much of the book's violence is, indeed, the brutality of Britain's exit from the subcontinent, in which millions migrated and several hundreds of thousands were killed. But the resulting lasting displacement, is harder to pin down. It is, in his own words, an "oceanic pain that traced its beginning to 1947", one that the poet sketches onto life in modern day America. 'My Mother's Darkness' evokes the city of Lyallpur, named after a British lieutenant governor of Punjab. The subsequent poem 'Faisalabad', Lyallpur's post-Partition name, contrasts the intimacy of home and kin against the defamiliarization of imperialist design and migration across real or spectral borders. Mohyuddin writes that to "rename a thing is an attempt to undo whatever unwantedness remains." But to be renamed is to always be doubled, inseparable from the past.

> Radiating outward from its circular heart
> are eight perfectly straight
> streets, like giant swords dividing the city
> into eight mohallas,
> each with its own name, its own magic
> and music. From above,
> from the vantage point
> of dead souls floating heavenward,
> the layout is a visual echo of the Union Jack,
> as if the British understood
> that to truly claim a place, it must be made
> in one's own image.

The inherited grief of these displaced children may not be as readily apparent to the uninitiated. Lyallpur was my own ancestral city so for me this book is astonishing. It is, however, a deeply necessary, clear and moving rejoinder to the silence of all our histories.

SANDEEP PARMAR

FAISAL MOHYUDDIN

The Displaced Children of Displaced Children begins with a nameless child, overwhelmed by longing, interviewing his father on matters of history, family and grief. Desperately wanting to feel closer to his father, each question emerges from a "bottomless" curiosity borne of the silences that pervade the child's life. Every response, expressed like a riddle, communicates the father's inability to answer. Thus, a shared sense of displacement frames the exchange, with both child and father seeking comfort and companionship in the other. Yet, in the end, both realize – as the reader might, too – that to find solace, and a sense of rootedness, they must turn their attention to the "untarnished majesty" of the future.

In my own life, the most uncomfortable silences, the ones I most longed to fill and which in turn ushered me heart-first into the poems that hold this book together, were those related to the unspoken, unrecorded traumas of the Partition of 1947. Poetry allowed me to invent imagined narratives about what my forbearers endured, cobble together answers to questions I could never voice, and forge a kinship with a host of displaced others (human or otherwise) to feel less lost. I could even – as I do in the opening poem – pull my father from death, mythologize him in the interview and broker a reconciliation with our pasts. The rest of the book meanders through time and space, from one body into another, resisting despair by turning again and again toward what is still possible.

Near the end of the collection, as if measuring my capacity to make peace with the "unknowability" of my own history, I hold a mirror up to my poet-self: "Do you remember, Faisal, what the elders preached about forgetting? Centuries of grief / Had made them wise, taught them to seek the mercy and goodness of mystery". Despite the pain and desperation that pervade so many of these poems, the book is ultimately an act of mercy, of forgiveness, of hope.

FAISAL RECOMMENDS

Layli Long Soldier, *WHEREAS* (Graywolf); Hari Alluri, *The Flayed City* (Kaya Press); Jack Ridl, *Losing Season* (CavanKerry); Patricia Smith, *Incendiary Art* (Triquarterly); Rajiv Mohabir, *The Cowherd's Son* (Tupelo); Leah Umansky, *The Barbarous Century* (Eyewear); Cynthia Dewi Oka, *Salvage* (Triquarterly); Mary Barbara Moore, *Amanda and the Man Soul* (Emrys); Leila Chatti, *Tunsiya/Amrikiya* (Bull City); Solmaz Sharif, *Look* (Graywolf); Chris Santiago, *Tula* (Milkweed); Kevin Coval, *A People's History of Chicago* (Haymarket); Patrick Rosal, *Brooklyn Antediluvian* (Persea); Javier Zamora, *Unaccompanied* (Copper Canyon Press).

Exile begins where rivers end....

A GHAZAL FOR THE DIASPORA

We have always been the displaced children of displaced children,
Tethered by distant rivers to abandoned lands, our blood's history lost.

To temper the grief, imagine your father's last breath as a Moghul garden—
Marble pool at its center, the mirrored sky holding all his tribe had lost.

Above the tussle of his wounded city, sad-eyed paper kites fight to stay aloft.
One lucky child will be crowned the winner, everyone else will have lost.

Wish peace upon every stranger who arrives at your door, even the thief—
For you never know when your last chance at redemption will be lost.

In another version of the story, a steady loneliness mothers away the rust.
Yet, without windows in its hull, the time-traveler's supplication gets lost.

Against flame-lipped testimonies of exile's erasures, the swinging of an axe.
Felled banyan trees populate your nightmares, new enlightenments lost.

The rim of this porcelain cup is chipped, so sip with practiced caution.
Even a trace of blood will copper the flavor, the respite of tea now lost.

Tell me, Faisal, with what new surrender can you evade deeper damnation?
Whatever it is, hack away, before your children too become the Lost.

JOHN KINSELLA

John Kinsella was born in Perth in 1963. He studied at the University of Western Australia and travelled extensively through Europe, the Middle East and Asia. He is the author of over twenty five books and has received a number of literary awards, including a Young Australian Creative Fellowship and a two-year Fellowship from the Literature Fund of the Australia Council. Since 1998 he has been International Editor for Arc Publications, with whom he has published four collections. His most recent collections include *The Hunt, Peripheral Light: Selected and New Poems, The New Arcadia* and *Shades of the Sublime & Beautiful.* He is a Fellow of Churchill College, Cambridge University, and a Research Fellow at the University of Western Australia.

THE WOUND

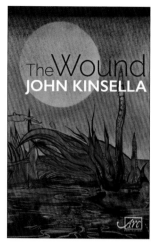

ARC | £10.99 | PBS PRICE £8.25

John Kinsella's ethical concerns as a poet-activist fearlessly constellate in *The Wound*. The central poem – a good portion of this book – reconfigures the myth of Sweeney, the Irish King sent mad by St. Ronan's curse to wander through his own land. Kinsella writes Sweeney into a devastated landscape threatened by climate change, land grabbing and deforestation. He looks at the behaviour behind our (in)action where, finally, Sweeney watches the rise of nationalism and human apathy. The King's madness is our own. Kinsella's is a tough, direct poetics, one that calls for action, for change. In 'Sweeney Deplores the Rise of the Fascists' the protagonist becomes witness, haunted by the hatred that, in turn, haunts us:

> by the toxins falling from the mouths of demagogues — angry
> whites who cherish the idea of DNA, swilling from chalices
>
> of pure hate, rallying around their flags gifted to them by
>   the warfare
> of their ancestors...

Elsewhere, there are remarkable versions of Friedrich Hölderlin, an "in conversation" as much as a kind of translation, engaging with the German poet whilst retaining Kinsella's own environmental concerns. As with the Sweeney poems, Kinsella cleverly echoes Hölderlin in order to emphasise a world on fire, at the brink of its own (self) destruction. At their most devastating, Kinsella's concerns feel prophetic and apocalyptic:

> When flames curl over the vineyard
> And a coal-fired wind
> Blackens the breathless hills,
> The colonial vineyard
> Just beyond town is a late summer
> Sentinel; grapes not set and bursting like fat cells;
> Fire wicking the vines as volunteers
> Fight off the harvest, notes of aroma.

With great tenancy and language, *The Wound* speaks to the anthropocentric age we live in, asking us if we are willing to change from polluting this "brittle air", before we plummet "deep into the wound, the graveyard, the deathzone".

SANDEEP PARMAR

| SELECTOR'S COMMENT

AFTER 'DER SOMMER' – 'WENN DANN VORBEI' DES FRÜHLINGS BLÜTHE SCHWINDET

THE SUMMER – WHEN THEN THE BLOSSOM OF SPRING VANISHES AWAY

The vanishing of back-when's spring-flowers,
Summer's now, entwining the year.
And, as through the valley, Toodyay Brook –
The ranges at full-stretch to hold it back.
Paddocks are exhausted but glassy-bright
With day, arching towards twilight;
And so the year hangs 'round, a summer's
Day for 'men' as impressions might fade with nature.

May 24th
1778.   Scardanelli

MICHAEL O'NEILL

Michael O'Neill was born in Aldershot in 1953 and moved to Liverpool in 1960. He read English at Exeter College, Oxford. Since 1979 he has lectured in English at Durham University, where he is a Professor of English and currently an Assistant Director of the Centre for Poetry and Poetics. He co-founded and co-edited *Poetry Durham* from 1982 to 1994. His recent critical books include, as co-author (with Michael D. Hurley), *Poetic Form: An Introduction* (Cambridge University Press, 2012). He received an Eric Gregory Award in 1983 for his poetry and a Cholmondeley Award for Poets in 1990. His two previous collections of poems are *The Stripped Bed* (Collins Harvill, 1990) and *Wheel* (Arc, 2008).

RETURN OF THE GIFT

ARC | £9.99 | PBS PRICE £7.50

Michael O'Neill's poems are shapely, personal, and they acknowledge his intelligence – he's an authority on Romantic poetry – without becoming academic or pretentious. There's a lovely early lyric, in 'The Stripped Bed', where the speaker pleads with his adopted infant to give over, so he can read some Keats: "Duplo Babels topple and rise again… //… I give Moneta up, then you a hug … // And now you're whisked, indignant, to the bath". O'Neill has cancer, and writes on this subject without mawkishness, or an engineered heroism:

> so in the course of my illness
> the fact that we love to crack jokes,
> to talk nonsense and pass
> into a private idiom
> may hint there's a hope that lurks
> in the disease's very medium

The delicate slant-rhymes ("illness" and "pass"; "jokes" and "lurks"; "idiom" and "medium") remind me of Seamus Heaney on Larkin – explaining that whenever a poem, however bleak, finds its true shape, it is on the side of life. We call verse like this courageous; an adjective one might also apply (more counter-intuitively) to 'Diversity'. Which concerns the experience of having assigned to you:

> Values that you didn't know you held
> – 'no, no', you bite back, 'not diversity,
> just courtesy'… All gone, failed –
>
> all gone, the culture of it, how we were and what it was,
> toughness, endurance, a way of making jokes…

O'Neill refuses political correctness in the name of an abiding decency – morals without need of legislation, unshackled by the tip-toe lexis of Human Resources. Some of us may, in these troubled times, have less faith in human nature than he does: reading his verse can help with this. Intelligently disgruntled, mildly inflamed, this seems to me a utopian poem. Humane and heartening, in its bafflement and embattlement.

FEBRUARY

Twilight beyond the fifteen-paned window
on the half-landing; twilight and a cold,
steady sky; you
staring at winter's outlines – spirits low

yet lifted by that air-built height,
lifted without much chance
of coming up with reasons for
embracing winter light,

there being no particular
reason to be glad trees should supplicate,
their branches stretched out so
you see through to a single star.

EVELYN SCHLAG

Evelyn Schlag was born and raised in Waidhofen an der Ybbs in Lower Austria. She studied German and English Literature at the University of Vienna and taught in Vienna for a time before returning to Waidhofen, where she divides her time between teaching and writing. She has written seven volumes of prose fiction, a book of essays and five collections of her own poetry.

ALL UNDER ONE ROOF
TRANSLATED BY KAREN LEEDER

CARCANET | £12.99 | PBS PRICE £9.75

Evelyn Schlag's *All Under One Roof*, translated by Karen Leeder, is a selection from two books subsequent to her 2009 *Selected Poems*. Leeder, in her introduction, talks of a voice that is "quiet, elegiac and largely inward, though it accommodates passion, grief and rage" adding that it is also "mysterious and humorous". The first poem in the book, 'Portrait of Cecilia Gallerani' is a funny, sharp contemplation of Leonardo da Vinci's 'Lady with the Ermine' by a detached observer on the difference between nature and art, between the ideal and the real. The beauty of it (in the translation) lies in the precision of tone and detail that opens onto a world of irony and ambiguity that is, nonetheless, serious and tender. Poems on politics, persona and place are treated with the same quizzical sharp-tenderness. There are poems of memory, vivid and personal, often using surreal juxtaposing, as in 'Indigo'

> I dream of indigo the way it used to be.
> Outline of the blueberry patch. The moose
> Fleeing the chalk and we had a word.
>
> Wilma fled school. Karina meat.
> We layered pine needles on top…

These jagged shifts move the poem forward beyond the moment into another state.

> [...] Next year
> the romantic countries will come over
> to our side. Into the gloom. Into the blue of walls.

We have entered a realm beyond the confines of the apparently simple theme. The power of the book lies in its ability constantly to move us further yet deeper. Leeder's language has a sinuosity and flow that is utterly convincing.

It was Schlag's (and Leeder's) lightness of touch that just about put her ahead of the excellent Doris Kareva, Mircea Dinescu and a very fine Grajaukas Gintaras.

GEORGE SZIRTES

VITA POETICA

It is long years since yesterday and how much I've
forgotten about those slow sentences in which I

leaned over sideways and a motive gave me my
answer it is long years since yesterday who had

such delicate fingers for questions when we'd
diagnose into the night: where is infra-blue slept

where in my tongues the star-streaked kept? I've got
running sand in my shoes from all the seven-liners

and where's the flooded eye of someone else? Long
years since yesterday who held my arm and stood

by me: you are a head beauty a Russian one
with a melancholy soul if I may make so bold on the

Nevsky? Long years of that tiny private picking
and back to back sharing a single air a tree.

MARY JEAN CHAN

Mary Jean Chan is a poet from Hong Kong. She was shortlisted for the 2017 Forward Prize for Best Single Poem, the 2016 *London Magazine* Poetry Prize and the 2016 Resurgence Poetry Prize (Commended), and is the winner of the 2017 Psychoanalysis and Poetry Competition, the 2017 Poetry Society Members' Poetry Competition and the 2016 Oxford Brookes International Poetry Competition (ESL). Mary Jean is an Editor at *Oxford Poetry*. Her debut collection is forthcoming from Faber & Faber (July 2019). She was recently awarded second place in the Poetry Society's National Poetry Competition.

A HURRY OF ENGLISH

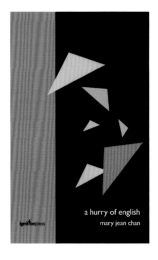

IGNITION   PRESS | £5.00

A Hurry of English' epigraph is from Audre Lorde: "when we are silent / we are still afraid". This quotation captures most of Mary Jean Chan's work: how she navigates through cultural differences to remind us that language is an agent of colonial history. "Red-Guarded days" and childhood memories flicker past as Chan wrestles with the notion of belonging and personal acceptance.

The opening poem sets up an intimate and appealing tone. 'Always' describes the generational rift between daughter and mother.

> Always the pen dreaming
> it could redeem the years
> you fled from, those
> Red-Guarded days
> and nightmares.

The poet attempts to reconnect with a fragmented inheritance. Here, lines thrive on word repetition.

I kept returning to 'Dress' and 'How It Must Be Said'. It is these prose poems that impress the most. 'Dress' is at once intimate and outward-looking. Tension between identity and queer encounters is explored with emotional clarity. Individual lines proceed forcefully, catching the reader's attention:

> your fingers brush the wrist of another girl as you jostle
> into the assembly hall, and you understand that sin was
> never meant to be easy, only sweet...

This all makes for a distinctive debut, in its blend of intimacy and desire. *A Hurry of English* is an accomplished body of work. Chan's poetry deserves to be read widely.

SELECTOR'S COMMENT

DENISE SAUL

LONG DISTANCE

You are running on the rain-dark pavement through Sutton Park. Where I am, sun. All the dehumidifiers are on in the house. No fireplaces. Some seas are colder than others, some bodies warmer. I am drinking Iron-Buddha: tea leaves waiting for their time to blossom. It is too spring here for my own good, too much green in the salad bowl. Too many stories of salvation; earlier, blue beyond belief. The moon is lying on its back in my dreams. What a smile looks like. A toothbrush touches my lips. Asian steamed sea bass for dinner, with white rice. Polar bears have black skin. Victoria Harbour was named after your Queen. How many hearts in a deck of cards shuffled across two continents? I am catching a plane tonight, thinking about the map on your neck.

ISN'T FOREVER | AMY KEY

AMY KEY

ISN'T FOREVER

BLOODAXE | £9.95 | PBS PRICE £7.47

In her second book-length collection *Isn't Forever* Amy Key explores the intricate and often aphonic elements of womanhood, femininity and aloneness. As the collection gathers momentum, the poems begin to display their necessary infighting while always managing to stay acutely performative on the page. The last couplet of the second poem 'I Do Not Need the Sea To Love Me Back' declares with aphoristic and stylistic exactness: "I waited for the sea to notice me / ~~But the sea never notices anyone~~." I kept returning to this underlying motif as I journeyed deeper into the book, absorbed and shaken by poems which can at times feel remotely existential while not appearing to be overly dependent on each other to exist.

Notions echoing desire, body image and love occupy warm and large sections of the book. Moments such as the one below found in the final stanza of the poem "How rare a really beautiful hand is now, since the harp has gone out of fashion!" pivots perfectly on the material world's symbolic tensions, while being batted against those of doubt and selfhood.

> Rose water — by the by I'd rather drink it
> as the hokey pendulum swings.
> I'm looking for something foolproof, aplomb
> that withstands the interrogating nude.

The poem 'Lousy with unfuckedness, I dream' which coincidently is the only piece that uses virgules, was the initial poem which brought Key's work to my attention after it was featured in the January 2018 edition of *Poetry*. Like much of Key's writing, we can expect to be met by a dexterous, fragmented and almost perfunctory world, which artfully circumnavigates moments so private it almost feels invasive to keep reading on, and that I feel is one of the poet's most remarkable abilities.

> ... we sleep together / hello
> cats / I make my bed daily / of the three types of
> hair on the sheets / only one is human...

ANTHONY ANAXAGOROU

ANTHONY ANAXAGOROU

Poetry can be many things. The PBS Wild Card is an important way of recognising radical, experimental and avant-garde styles of writing which help progress the form...

ANTHONY ANAXAGOROU has published nine volumes of poetry, a spoken-word EP and a collection of short stories. His work has appeared on BBC Newsnight, Radio 4, ITV and Sky Arts as well as being published in *The Feminist Review*, Amnesty International's *Words That Burn* and John Berger's anthology *The Long White Thread of Words*. He was commissioned by the Labour Party during the 2017 general election to write their campaign poem. In 2015 he won the Groucho Maverick Award and in 2016 he was shortlisted for the Hospital Club's H-100 award for influential people. In 2012 he founded Out-Spoken, London's premier poetry and music night, and Out-Spoken Press, an independent publisher which challenges the lack of diversity in British publishing.

WILD CARD SELECTOR

AMY KEY

The poems I wrote as I put the book together are both in search of, and a resistance to settling on, selfhood. I think if there were to be an engine for the poems it would be fuelled by this Sappho fragment (translated by Anne Carson):

> I don't know what to do
> > two states of mind in me

And this from Maggie Nelson's 'The Argonauts':

> I was ashamed, but undaunted (my epithet?).

That is to say I am interested in the slipperiness of personal identity and even physical boundaries (seeking "a finger-touch confirming my edges"), contrariness and how shame drives not only how we feel and the beliefs we hold about ourselves, but also our actions. When I think about the book, rather than any direct poetic influence, it is these concerns that come to mind. I guess I believe that being yourself – a kind of "fixed ideal" of *you-ness* – is a hokey notion and one that is commodified and sold as the answer to our personal challenges.

The other major influence for the poems is the sea, specifically the sea as a conductor for self knowledge and achieving an elusive interiority. In one of the poems, the line "Tell me where the sea ends & the sky begins Ha! You cannot" might as well be about the feeling of *becoming* the sea, giving the self up to it (sea as a magic trick, "as a cauldron / I'm making spells in"), as it is about not being able to trust what one is seeing.

AMY RECOMMENDS

Fran Lock, *Dogtooth* (Out-Spoken Press); Oki Sogumi, *Poems 2012-2017* (Face Press); Patricia Smith, *Incendiary Art* (Triquarterly Books); A.K. Blakemore, *Fondue* (Offord Road Books); Eds. Rachael Boast, Andy Ching, Nathan Hamilton (Editors) *The Caught Habits of Language: An Entertainment for W.S. Graham for Him Having Reached One Hundred* (Donut Press); Natalie Eilbert, *Indictus* (Noemi Press); Kathryn Maris, *The House With Only an Attic And a Basement* (Penguin); Momtaza Mehri, *Sugah. Lump. Prayer.* (Akashic Books); Emily Hasler, *The Built Environment* (Pavilion), Richard Scott, *Soho* (Faber & Faber; Makoto Ueda (Editor and Translator), *Far Beyond the Field: Haiku by Japanese Women* (Columbia University Press).

AMY KEY grew up in Kent and the North-East and now lives in London. Her first collection *Luxe* was published by Salt in 2013. She is the author of two pamphlets *Instead of Stars* (Tall Lighthouse) and *History* (If A Leaf Falls Press). In 2014 she edited an anthology of poems on friendship between women *Best Friends Forever* (The Emma Press) and co-edited the online journal *Poems in Which*. Her poems have been widely published in magazines and anthologies including *Poetry, The Poetry Review, New Statesman, Granta, Best British Poetry 2015* (Salt), *Poetry Please* (Faber & Faber) and *The Poetry of Sex* (Penguin).

WILD CARD CHOICE

Image: Sophie Davidson

PBS STUDENT POETRY PRIZE

Reading for a poetry competition such as this sets a particular challenge because each poem, stripped of any of the extra-poetic context we are used to, must work as a discrete unit. It must go somewhere economically but absolutely in its short space, without any additional information for the reading about what went into the poet or the poem's life.

'Scattering' appeared to me on first sight as a poem without scaffold or runway leading up to it: not only in a superficial sense because it effectively uses the wandering and continuous prose line within those tight margins, but because it felt, from the beginning, like a singular act of articulation, as though it could be said only one way, this way. Phrases stand alone as "bulletin pip[s]" but make up a sequence of memory and recurrence both inevitable and unpredictable.

'Agarbatti' makes a questioning art of a phone's autocorrect function: the serendipitous alignment between words is used to prise apart the language and to forge a rich emotional tenor.

And in 'The Civic Sinking Society', a decisive and freely imaginative view of a Cumbrian landscape finds room to roam in long and confident lines which nonetheless return, in each paragraph, to cycles of life, natural and otherwise.

- Sam Buchan-Watts

ABOUT THE JUDGE

Sam Buchan-Watts is co-editor of the poetry press clinic. His pamphlet was published in 2016 in the Faber New Poets series and he won an Eric Gregory Award the same year. He was, until recently, Reviews Editor for *Poetry London*.

JUDGE'S COMMENTS

THE WINNERS

1ST PRIZE

JAY G YING

UNIVERSITY OF EDINBURGH (MEDICINE)

2ND PRIZE

ALYCIA PIRMOHAMED

UNIVERSITY OF EDINBURGH (CREATIVE WRITING)

3RD PRIZE

ILA COLLEY

UNIVERSITY OF EDINBURGH (ARCHITECTURE)

HIGHLY COMMENDED POEMS

FISH MARKET
WENDY MIN JI CHOI
UNIVERSITY COLLEGE LONDON

VIADUCT
MARIAH WHELAN
UNIVERSITY OF MANCHESTER

LEVIATHAN
OLIVER TONG
UNIVERSITY OF ABERDEEN

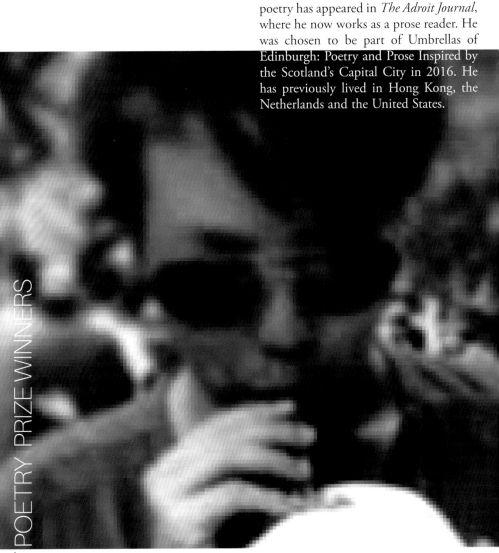

JAY G. YING studies medicine at the University of Edinburgh. His prose-poetry has appeared in *The Adroit Journal*, where he now works as a prose reader. He was chosen to be part of Umbrellas of Edinburgh: Poetry and Prose Inspired by the Scotland's Capital City in 2016. He has previously lived in Hong Kong, the Netherlands and the United States.

STUDENT POETRY PRIZE WINNERS

SCATTERING

for him I tried hard to pull
together this orange; from
the mandarins' testament
in the sink, a segment of
the new globe unpeels in
my mind. Each bulletin pip
picked like a memory from
the pulp of what remains:
earth in earth. In earth, in a
dream, a golem's hand
lopsided, half buried like a
stem from a glass, half of
an inert ritual. Keeping
house, his fingers churned
the clay; gulleting in the
tall grass, the fat egrets
waited by the stream for
their sweet breads; in the
wind blue was the tang
from a piece of seed. As I
remembered his image
from the page he unshapes
it; like silt in a river that
returns to dust, he is
displaced. Zest from a
tangerine or a clementine;
Taiwan, Tangier. Like men
each world opens with a
knife; inside I find a sweet
receipt, its paper slip, the
word I do not know
anymore—what had he
said to me: Prodigal, what
were your wanderings
about

JAY G. YING

58

ALYCIA PIRMOHAMED is a Canadian-born poet completing a Ph.D. at the University of Edinburgh on poetry by second-generation immigrant writers. Her writing explores what it means to be the daughter of immigrants and grapples with language loss, cultural identity and displacement. Her work appeared in the 2018 *Best New British and Irish Poets* anthology. Alycia received an MFA from the University of Oregon.

As an emerging writer, it means a lot to have this opportunity to share my work. I hope this poem resonates with readers.

AGARBATTI

Agarbatti autocorrects to *aggravate*

and I realize that I am
an electrical current—

aggravated.

My father
lit the bamboo every day

while I was learning to forget my
First Language

at the elementary school
down the street.

I returned to smoke and calm
and a strange loss

emptiness like clockwork

my body void of its vowels, my mouth
pricked

with the metallic taste of this country.

Did agarbatti help

my father who diligently set ablaze
the masala tip alongside

the coo of his favourite radio show?

Or was it aggravate? This tall, gentle man
who possessed a red lick of fire

until the Paxil
settled in. Until each elliptical

seed
cracked open and coaxed his spirit

into a thick fog
I would always return to.

*Agarbatti: incense in India. Paxil: antidepressant drug

ILA COLLEY is an Architecture student at the University of Edinburgh. Her poetry has been published in *Butcher's Dog* and *hotdog*. She was a two-time winner of the Foyle Young Poets award and is also a Writing Squad graduate.

I'm so happy to be placed in this competition; 'The Civic Sinking Society' was written in pieces and catalogues a geography of growing older in unplanned ways.

THE CIVIC SINKING SOCIETY

In the eternal Craggy Wood ropes shrug from shoulders that are unnerved
by the punctuality of dawn who is laying the table with hay bales
and drystone linings. here is a tired eyelid. you will not draw this postcard
though the weight of a line turns you on. instead you are looking into the abyss
of a traffic light following its predetermined cycle. every Monday
there is a chance to end it all in the estuary of a coffee shop where the bearded man
consumes himself and you pay a pretty penny to see. you think he would love you
if he knew how to crop and resize without losing quality: enlarge you
from a thread to a thigh, the quick transmission of cold glass keeping the cakes
correctly inflated. blush and remember your predetermined cycle. the weight
of a line carries both ways, you are a complex system of pipes, a vessel that is brief
and endless. you are not a river and yet you will take what you are given.

Soon, over Staveley, the sky will clot and Craggy, the giant head of broccoli
that looms over the recreation ground, over the varicosing valleyward river,
will send its condolences to Gowan Terrace with one pulmonary refurbishment
to its canopy. it is precisely this kind of disaster that has all the drains gaping
on a Saturday. your mother sends an sms from underwater, you are so distraught
you leave Jeff Buckley mid-croon on the no. 2, headed for the coast and back,
following its predetermined cycle. you pay a pretty penny to see his face again.
he loves you and he is dead: this is not coincidence. now all your dreams
are funerary topographies, a database of love lost, the Victorian premature;
each thumbnail a headstone or the other way around. in a reply to your mother
you point out that we are all immortal, there is no point in dying anyway.
she says the river took the last bridge, *I'm out of milk, I'm stranded*. moses wept.

Behind Bluebell Wood something is being kept alight while the water unshelves
hundreds of skimming stones, stuns the civic picket, slips under the covers
of coppice land; the village is an abandoned scratch card. but all you can think of is Jeff,
a whole weekend shacked up in somebody else's pocket. he's a changed man,
paranoid, his promises carry both ways. it's Monday again and you want to end it all
but just minimise him: a thumbnail, a forgotten fever. blush your way back to reality,
pay a penny to rattle the pipes: a bearded man touches you through a cold glass
cabinet, from a thigh to a thread. you are a river, you are not an institute but a bounty,
the street shadows you like an uncertain electrocardiograph. you stammer down
the phone "*Yes, life is a heavy burden!*" nothing is given, everything is taken.
your mother lays the table, following her predetermined cycle. it will be a long time
before you go home. the village will be an estuary. there will be a garage
and a coffee shop. the room will open like a greetings card: *condolences*.

ILA COLLEY

NEW BOOKS

WAKE: GILLIAN ALLNUTT

Allnut's verse is sparse, characterised by a taut rhythmic snap, the evocation of grand depths of meaning alluded to with the most economical of language. *wake* is like a surface layer of archaeological findings giving a tantalising glimpse into a great, expansive history. This collection is certainly historical, the poems brushing against pasts both distant and immediate. All are graced by a fine, contemplative, tragic sensibility.

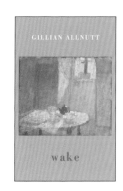

BLOODAXE BOOKS | £9.95 | PBS PRICE £7.47

DIRTY LAUNDRY: DEBORAH ALMA

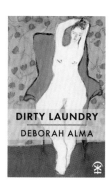

A sense of the rural gothic pervades this collection, the poet's voice moving episodically through pastoral and domestic environments at once inviting and unnerving. The direction these poems take meanders through the darkly humorous and the ribald, through catalogues of lovers, memories of people and places. Alma seems to suggest that the mundane and the everyday are never simply that; a rich, unsettling, transcendent power underscores our collated experiences.

NINE ARCHES PRESS | £9.99 | PBS PRICE £7.50

THE BUILT ENVIRONMENT: EMILY HASLER

Hasler reveals an infectious fascination with how things are put together. In its purest form this is structural, architectural, but Hasler's pen works its way down further to chemical processes. Craftwork is examined and the way in which culture is inscribed upon material goods and the world around us; ideology is engraved upon objects from memorial plaques to swords and even into the living, breathing world. This is an intriguing, deft collection, demonstrating Hasler's spellbinding ability to make the material world leap from the page.

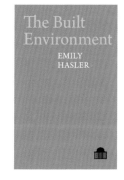

PAVILION POETRY | £9.99 | PBS PRICE £7.50

LEDBURY GUEST REVIEWERS

BLACKBIRD, BYE BYE: MONIZA ALVI
REVIEWED BY JENNIFER LEE TSAI

Alvi's new collection is inspired by her parents, her Pakistani father's immigration and imbued with "the long enchantment" of loss. As "the owl-artist, delineating each feather", Alvi's poignant, delicate and fantastical poems imagine the lives and afterlives of "Motherbird" and "Fatherbird" with tender restraint and whimsical fancy. The theme of birds extends to versions of poems by French poets Jules Supervielle and Saint-John Perse and poems "after" the Spanish-Mexican surrealist artist Remedios Varo.

BLOODAXE BOOKS | £9.95 | PBS PRICE 7.47

BUTTERFLY VALLEY: SHERKO BEKAS, TRANS. CHOMAN HARDI
REVIEWED BY MARYAM HESSAVI

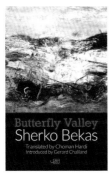

This book-length epic finds its wings pinned in the pages of the delicate imagination that is Sherko Bekas' *Butterfly Valley*. As "drop by drop the rain writes flowers", we flutter through the "bright sorrows" and tragedies of 20th century Kurdistan, of exile, resistance, loneliness, "colourful daydreams" and astonishing moonlit hope. Nowhere else have I felt myth and history attended with such unashamedly sharp splendour, whilst holding such a clear mirror up to our contemporary human state.

ARC | £10.99 | PBS PRICE £8.25

ENGLAND: POEMS FROM A SCHOOL: ED. KATE CLANCHY
REVIEWED BY SRISHTI KRISHNAMOORTHY-CAVELL

This anthology of poems by Oxford Spires Academy pupils offers a vibrant collage of distinctive voices performing complex I-work that transcends the enclosed biographies of the young poets. The poems negotiate the pressures of speaking about home and foreignness, the anxiety of inheritance and identity, by finding one's astonishing way through new, old and composite languages and landscapes. The writing blossoms – luminous in its testimony and striking in its evocation of memories.

PICADOR | £9.99 | PBS PRICE £7.50

BOOK REVIEWS

LEDBURY GUEST REVIEWERS

This powerful first collection surprises at every turn. In inventive, witty, deeply poignant and accessible poems, Corcoran makes the familiar unfamiliar, the political personal and vice versa. Addressing a dazzling array of themes – from the traditional subjects of family, love and loss, to police failings, a romantic rendezvous with Sonny Corleone and a satirical exploration of the pro-Brexit slogan "Take Back Control" – this is a compelling portrait of contemporary Britain. An essential read.

NINE ARCHES PRESS | £9.99 | PBS PRICE £7.50

A PERFECT MIRROR: SARAH CORBETT
REVIEWED BY JADE CUTTLE

A Perfect Mirror flickers more secrets about the Calder Valley into view than a mirror ever could. Marvelling at moss and the moon of ice, elsewhere plying the mystery of puddles, these miraculous poems nurse the glint of sun into gold. Even the sky begins to speak, graced by the ghosts of Wordsworth, Plath, Bronte and Austen, as scaling each hill entails a hike into the imagination, "where the mind goes gliding beyond the shores of its ocean... moving towards a horizon we will never touch".

PAVILION POETRY | £9.99 | PBS PRICE £7.50

NEW POETRIES VII: ED. MICHAEL SCHMIDT
REVIEWED BY NASSER HUSSAIN

New Poetries VII carries on the excellent Carcanet tradition of introducing readers to some of the best poets in the UK today. The twenty-two poets included in this anthology are a diverse mix, and anthologies can overwhelm – so the short introductions from each writer is a considerate touch. Each one is a warm welcome into the processes that underwrite the many wonderful poems to be found here. One highlight is Zohar Atkins' reworking of Walt Whitman, but there's plenty more.

CARCANET | £12.99 | PBS PRICE £9.75

STUDENT REVIEWERS

ESSEX CLAY: ANDREW MOTION
REVIEWED BY ANNAH RIDDELL

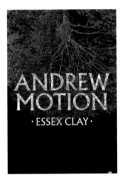

Essex Clay is a wonderful and captivating narrative that compels the reader to delve further. As the story develops, we are enveloped in the minds of the novel-like characters. The tragic theme and the *bildungsroman* style inspire us to observe our own memories of youth and experiences of grief, hardship and belonging, as well as the fleeting nature of life.

FABER & FABER | £14.99 | PBS PRICE £11.25

SOHO: RICHARD SCOTT
REVIEWED BY JULIA MCGEE-RUSSELL

A raw depiction of love and abuse, Richard Scott's debut collection *Soho* is both unflinchingly sensual and quietly devastating. Full of innuendos and blatant sexuality, this four-part compilation of poems is a battle cry for "the homosexual you / cannot be proud of". With beautifully savage imagery and dry, self-aware wit, this is a call against shame, ending in an ode to "Silver-crowning Soho".

FABER | £10.99 | PBS PRICE £8.25

IMMIGRANT: USHA KISHORE
REVIEWED BY JENNIFER SZANDROWSKA

A beautiful exploration of the limits and possibilities of language, as an immigrant in Britain. Kishore captures the feeling of disloyalty behind composing poetry in the colonisers' language – "desi poets appropriating your imperial tongue" – as well as the need to reclaim this. There is a nostalgic ache throughout the collection for the India the British Empire destroyed and a call to forge a truly integrated Britain; addressing race, language, religion, cultural appropriation and the literary canon, *Immigrant* is a challenging but compelling read.

EYEWEAR PUBLISHING | £10.99 | PBS PRICE £8.25

BOOK REVIEWS

PAMPHLETS

PAMPER ME TO HELL & BACK: HERA LINDSAY BIRD

A master of the absurdist simile and the non-sequitur, Hera Lindsay Bird delivers a deeply funny pamphlet in her unique poetic voice. Reading it is like observing a cynic extract ribbons of bad television lines and pop culture references from a shredder and then have a semi-ironic romantic epiphany. Dark, crude, flippant, extremely self-aware and consistently surprising, this anarchic collection is a joy to read.

SMITH | DOORSTOP BOOKS | £7.50 |

TROUPERS: KEITH HUTSON

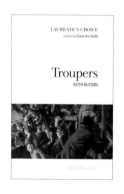

An odyssey across show and stage, chronicling the lives (and deaths) of performers over more than a century, *Troupers* is not a simple paean. The nature of entertainment, the consequences of the entertainer's life and the relationship between performer and audience come under observation in Hutson's clear-eyed and dextrous verse. The neologistic title, combining the performing troupe with military troopers, sharply encapsulates the mental and physical toll placed upon those who dedicate their lives to entertaining the crowd. A fascinating and troubling portrait of the curious celebrities of yesteryear.

SMITH | DOORSTOP | £7.50 |

BOG ARABIC: BERNADETTE McCARTHY

A compelling meditation on otherness, language and culture, McCarthy composes innovative representations of Irish and Arabic identity. This multicultural project blends identities which would superficially seem incompatible, examining the facets of difference. The pamphlet is given further weight by its deft, muscular verse and by McCarthy's talent for evoking vivid environments within which her ideas can be fully explored.

SOUTHWORD EDITIONS | £5.00 |

PAMPHLETS

In the guise of a monograph, this experimental sequence is arranged as an A-Z of theoretical phobias and mental conditions arising from the current Digital Age. Half playful and half troubling, Mierscheid's uncanny list (backed up by a wonderfully falsified bibliography and spurious academic credentials) has the disarming effect of occasionally, and sharply, touching upon familiar psychological quirks.

NEON   BOOKS | £4.00 |

BEZDELKI: CAROL RUMENS

The Emma Press delivers another beautifully illustrated collection, featuring poems and translations dedicated to the memory of translator Yuri Drobyshev. A reflection upon memory and the mortal condition, Rumens draws from a range of cultural touchstones, including historical imaginings of the afterlife. A moving and thought-provoking pamphlet.

THE   EMMA   PRESS | £5.00 |

THIRTY POETS GO TO THE GYM: GEORGE SZIRTES

Szirtes humorously slips into the stylistic skins of thirty famous poets to navigate the trials and tribulations of treadmills, barbells and rowing machines. Poets from Blake to Plath can be found sweating under weights and bemoaning their footwear within the confines of the gymnasium. A parodic pastiche not just of poetry but of the gym-going ethic, this wonderful pamphlet is completed by a send-up of the author himself, penned by Martin Figura.

CANDLESTICK   PRESS | £6.95 |

PBS PRESENTS

PBS SOUTHBANK SUMMER SHOWCASE

PBS Book Selector and Ledbury Forte Poetry prize-winner Sandeep Parmar hosts the PBS Summer Showcase at the Southbank Centre to launch the Summer *Bulletin* with readings by our Wild Card Choice Amy Key, Pamphlet Choice Mary Jean Chan and Student Poetry Prize winner, Jay G. Ying. Join us for a sizzling hot summer's evening of poetry from some of the most exciting new voices on the poetry scene today.

25th July | 7.30pm | £10 | Southbank Centre | London

NORTHERN POETRY SYMPOSIUM
CROSSINGS : TRANSLATION

© Sean Scully Untitled, 1967

3RD MAY | SAGE | GATESHEAD
WWW.NEWCASTLEPOETRYFESTIVAL.CO.UK

SUMMER LISTINGS

NEW BOOKS

AUTHOR	TITLE	PUBLISHER	RRP
Gillian Allnutt	wake	Bloodaxe Books	£9.95
Deborah Alma	Dirty Laundry	Nine Arches Press	£9.99
Moniza Alvi	Blackbird, Bye Bye	Bloodaxe Books	£9.95
Virginia Astley	The English River	Bloodaxe Books	£12.00
John Barnie	Departure Lounge	Cinnamon Press	£8.99
David Batten	Untergang	Cinnamon Press	£8.99
Cathy Bryant	Erratics	Arachne Press	£8.99
Helen Burke, Ed. Jamie McGarry	Today the Birds Will Sing	Valley Press	£30.00
Vahni Capildeo	Venus as a Bear	Carcanet Press	£9.99
J.R. Carpenter	An Ocean of Static	Penned in the Margins	£9.99
Keith Chandler	The Goldsmith's Apprentice	Fair Acre Press	£9.99
Kate Clanchy (Ed.)	England: Poems from a School	Picador	£9.99
Loretta Collins Klobah	Ricantations	Peepal Tree Press	£9.99
Sarah Corbett	A Perfect Mirror	Pavilion Poetry	£9.99
Josephine Corcoran	What Are You After?	Nine Arches Press	£9.99
Ailbhe Darcy	Insistence	Bloodaxe Books	£9.95
Aviva Dautch, Romalyn Ante and Sarala Estruch	Primers Volume 3	Nine Arches Press	£9.99
Kate Davis	The Girl Who Forgets How to Walk	Penned in the Margins	£9.99
John F. Deane	Dear Pilgrims	Carcanet Press	£9.99
Theo Dorgan	Orpheus	Dedalus Press	£10.00
Tishani Doshi	Girls Are Coming Out of the Woods	Bloodaxe Books	£9.95
Frank Dullaghan	Lifting the Latch	Cinnamon Press	£8.99
Martina Evans	Now We Can Talk Openly About Men	Carcanet Press	£9.99
Kate Foley	A Gift of Rivers	Arachne Press	£8.99
Mark Ford	Enter, Fleeing	Faber & Faber	£10.99
Giles Goodland	The Masses	Shearsman Books	£9.95
James Harpur	The White Silhouette	Carcanet Press	£11.99
Emily Hasler	The Built Environment	Pavilion Poetry	£9.99
Martin Hayes	Roar!	Smokestack Books	£7.99
Norbert Hirschhorn	Stone. Bread. Salt.	Holland Park Press	£8.00
Will Holloway	Better than Paradise	Smokestack Books	£7.99
Alex Houen	Ring Cycle	Eyewear Publishing	£10.99
Sarah Jackson and Tim Youngs (Eds.)	In Transit	The Emma Press	£10.00
Amy Key	Isn't Forever	Bloodaxe Books	£9.95
John Kinsella	The Wound	Arc Publications	£10.99
Usha Kishore	Immigrant	Eyewear Publishing	£10.99
Sue Leigh	Chosen Hill	Two Rivers Press	£9.99
Julia Rose Lewis	Phenomenology of the Feral	Knives Forks & Spoons	£11.00
Tim Liardet	Arcimboldo's Bulldog: New and Selected Poems	Carcanet Press	£14.99
Kathryn Maris	The House with only an Attic and a Basement	Penguin	£7.99
Ian McDonald	Collected Poems	Peepal Tree Press Ltd	£17.99
Alice Miller	Nowhere Nearer	Pavilion Poetry	£9.99
Faisal Mohyuddin	The Displaced Children Of Displaced Children	Eyewear Publishing	£10.99
J.O. Morgan	Assurances	Jonathan Cape	£10.00
Andrew Motion	Essex Clay	Faber & Faber	£14.99
Sean O'Brien	Europa	Picador	£9.99

SUMMER LISTINGS

AUTHOR	TITLE	PUBLISHER	RRP
John O'Donnell	Sunlight: New & Selected Poems	Dedalus Press	£12.00
Michael O'Neill	Return of the Gift	Arc Publications	£9.99
Bobby Parker	Working Class Voodoo	Offord Road Books	£10.00
Elizabeth Parker	In Her Shambles	Seren	£9.99
Vaughan Pilikian	Book of Days	Mica Press	£9.99
Robert Powell	Riverain	Valley Press	£10.99
Peter Raynard	Precarious	Smokestack Books	£7.99
Colin Campbell Robinson	Blue Solitude	Knives Fork & Spoons	£10.00
David Rushmer	Remains to be Seen	Shearsman Books	£10.95
Lesley Saunders	Nominy Dominy	Two Rivers Press	£9.99
Stephen Sawyer	There Will Be No Miracles Here	Smokestack Books	£7.99
Richard Scott	Soho	Faber & Faber	£10.99
Clare Shaw	Flood	Bloodaxe Books	£9.95
Tracy K. Smith	Wade in the Water	Penguin	£8.99
Matthew Sweeney	My Life as a Painter	Bloodaxe Books	£9.95
Leah Umansky	The Barbarous Century	Eyewear Publishing	£10.99
Lydia Unsworth	Certain Manoeuvres	Knives Forks & Spoons	£9.00
Claire Williamson	Visiting the Minotaur	Seren	£9.99
Joseph Woods	Monsoon Diary	Dedalus Press	£10.50

TRANSLATIONS

AUTHOR	TITLE	PUBLISHER	RRP
Sherko Bekas, trans. Choman Hardi	Butterfly Valley	Arc Publications	£10.99
Mircea Dinescu, trans. Adam J. Sorkin & Lidia Vianu	The Barbarians' Return	Bloodaxe Books	£12.00
Kristiina Ehin, trans. Ilmar Lehtpere	On the Edge of a Sword	Arc Publications	£10.99
Gintaras Grajauskas, trans. Rimas Uzgiris	Then What	Bloodaxe Books	£9.95
Vasily Kandinsky, trans. Tony Frazer	Sounds	Shearsman Books	£14.95
Doris Kareva, trans. Miriam McIlfatrick-Ksenofontov	Days of Grace	Bloodaxe Books	£12.00
Gerdur Kristny, trans. Rory McTurk	Drapa	Arc Publications	£10.99
Carita Nyström, Marko Hautala & Ralf Andtbacka	Kolme|Tre	Smith|Doorstop	£6.00
Evelyn Schlag, trans. Karen Leeder	All Under One Roof	Carcanet Press	£12.99